谨以此书致敬中华人民共和国成立75周年

这里是
中国石油

图书在版编目（CIP）数据

这里是中国石油 / 中国石油报社编 . -- 北京：石油工业出版社, 2025.3. -- ISBN 978-7-5183-7339-0

Ⅰ . F426.22-64

中国国家版本馆 CIP 数据核字第 2025LB5372 号

这里是中国石油

中国石油报社　编

出版发行：石油工业出版社

　　　　　（北京市朝阳区安华里二区 1 号楼 100011）

网　　址：www.petropub.com

编 辑 部：(010) 64523631　图书营销中心：(010) 64523633

印　　刷：北京雅昌艺术印刷有限公司

2025 年 3 月第 1 版　2025 年 3 月第 1 次印刷

710 毫米 ×1000 毫米　开本：1/16　印张：8.75

字数：30 千字

定　价：120.00 元

（如发现印装质量问题，我社图书营销中心负责调换）

版权所有，翻印必究

编委会

主　任　　霍恚明
副主任　　齐金蓉
主　编　　耿玉锋
副主编　　高照 李向阳 薛梅
编　辑　　金添 卞昌松 张旭 胡冰 刘红梅 李佳奇

Editorial Board

Director/Huo Huiming
Deputy Director/Qi Jinrong
Chief Editor/Geng Yufeng
Deputy Chief Editors/Gao Zhao　Li Xiangyang　Xue Mei
Editors/Jin Tian　Bian Changsong　Zhang Xu　Hu Bing　Liu Hongmei　Li Jiaqi

目录 CONTENTS

阳春布德泽，万物生光辉。
机器的轰鸣与春的韵律交织，
汇成油气生产的进行曲。
员工穿梭其间，仿佛被春的活力注入身体，
正以饱满的热情开启
"我为祖国献石油"的新征程。

005

力尽不知热，但惜夏日长。
比盛夏还酷热的，
是那烈日下的石油热情；
它具象为脉脉朝晖，
照耀着"奔向世界一流"的
砥砺之路！

043

喜看稻菽千重浪，遍地英雄下夕烟。
秋日将天空铺满金黄，
大地献出收获的宝藏，
石油的齿轮，在秋的深处，
与生命的节律同频咬合。

075

千里冰封，万里雪飘。
石油人在白色荒原，
以寒为笔，以雪作画，
点染出独属于自己的热血丹青；
他们用石油工业的春暖花开，
为每个冬日写下最后的句点！

107

大家长期在艰苦的环境下工作，挑战生命禁区，任劳任怨、默默付出，为我国的油气勘探开发、西气东输作出了重要贡献，功不可没！

能源安全关系我国经济社会发展全局，是最重要的安全之一。当前，我国正处于冬季用能高峰期。各地区各部门要认真落实党中央决策部署，坚持全国"一盘棋"，精心组织调度，全力做好煤电油气保供稳价工作，做好应对极端寒潮天气的准备，守住民生用能底线，确保群众温暖过冬。中央企业是能源保供的"顶梁柱"，要进一步提高政治站位，增强责任感和使命感，多措并举全力增产保供，确保经济社会发展用能需求。

——2023年1月18日，习近平总书记在北京通过视频连线看望慰问中国石油塔里木油田基层干部员工

轮南油气储运中心西气东输第一站克拉集气区。
It is the Kela Gas Gathering Area, the first station of the West-East Gas Transmission at Lunnan Oil & Gas Storage and Transportation Center.

4

春

SPRING

春雨惊春清谷天

"我为祖国献石油"的新征程。正以饱满的热情开启员工穿梭其间,仿佛被春的活力注入身体,汇成油气生产的进行曲。机器的轰鸣与春的韵律交织,阳春布德泽,万物生光辉。

实现绿色低碳转型,加快油气勘探开发与新能源融合发展,是贯彻落实习近平生态文明思想的生动实践,是高质量保障能源供应和油气核心需求的重要举措,必须以系统观念、工程思维正确处理好能源绿色低碳转型过程中各类关系和挑战,久久为功、善作善成。力争到本世纪中叶新能源产能达到两亿吨油当量,占公司国内能源总产能的"半壁江山",再造一个"绿色中国石油"。

——中国石油集团党组书记、董事长戴厚良

春天的塔里木,夺油上产满弓劲发。

  2021 年以来，中国石油在长江经济带企业以实际行动助力大江大河生态环境持续改善。位于长江畔的西北销售公司武汉油库，成为武汉市首家具备油船生活废水、含油废水接收和处理能力的企业。

Since 2021, CNPC's enterprises in the Yangtze River Economic Belt have taken practical actions to help continuously improve the ecological environment of major rivers. The Wuhan Oil Depot of the Northwest Marketing Company, located on the banks of the Yangtze River, has become the first enterprise in Wuhan with the capability to receive and treat domestic wastewater and oily wastewater from oil tankers.

中国石油通过建立重点流域及海域废水排污口管理清单等措施维护黄河生态环境安全。地处黄河上游的兰州石化公司连续多年被评为中国石油环境保护先进企业。

CNPC maintains the ecological and environmental safety of the Yellow River through the establishment of a management list of sewage outlets in key watersheds and sea areas, along with pertinent measures. Lanzhou Petrochemical Company, which is located in the upper reaches of the Yellow River, has been recognized as CNPC's advanced enterprise in environmental protection for multiple consecutive years.

2023年2月,西南油气田蓬深6井顺利完钻,井深达到9026米,刷新当时亚洲最深直井纪录。

In February 2023, the Well Pengshen-6 in the Southwest Oil & Gas Field Company was successfully drilled to a depth of 9,026 meters, setting a new record for the deepest vertical well in Asia at that time.

以广东石化为核心"链主",中国石油在南海之畔串联起一条化工产业链,有力推动粤港澳大湾区及其周边区域协同发展。

With Guangdong Petrochemical as the core of the "chain master", CNPC has facilitated the establishment of a chemical industry chain on the shore of the South China Sea, strongly promoting the synergistic development of the Guangdong-Hong Kong-Macao Greater Bay Area and its neighboring regions.

长庆油田的华 H100 平台是目前亚洲陆上最大页岩油水平井平台，用 30 亩的占地面积撬动着地下 4 万亩的资源。

The Hua H100 platform in the Changqing Oilfield is currently the largest onshore shale oil horizontal well platform in Asia. It occupies a land area of 30 mu (a Chinese unit of area, approximately 2 hectares) to access 40,000 mu (approximately 2,666.67 hectares) of subterranean oil resources.

春耕期间，为满足农耕大型机械用油需求，四川销售德阳分公司员工送油到德新镇五星村。

During the spring ploughing, to meet the oil demand of large farming machinery, employees of Sichuan Deyang Sales Branch of CNPC sent oil to Wuxing Village in Dexin Town.

面对清洁能源消费转型,近年来,上海销售公司建成投运了公司首座油氢合建站、首座纯氢站、首座含分布式光伏发电并网的综合能源服务站。

Facing the transformation of clean energy consumption, in recent years, Shanghai Marketing Company has built and put into operation the company's first gasoline and hydrogen filling station, the first pure hydrogen station and the first integrated energy service station with distributed photovoltaic power generation connected to the grid.

中国石油在哈萨克斯坦投建的奇姆肯特炼厂在大力推动当地经济建设的同时,让"绿色生产"贯穿始终。

The Shymkent refinery, invested in and built by CNPC in Kazakhstan, has been vigorously promoting the local economic construction while consistently implementing "green production" throughout its operations.

多年来，南方勘探公司始终坚持"油田开发到哪，绿化就建设到哪"，为当地生态保护作出重要贡献。

Over the years, China Southern Petroleum Exploration & Development Corporation has consistently adhered to the principle of "wherever the oilfield is developed, the greening will be constructed". This commitment has made significant contributions to local ecological protection.

辽河油田加快推进保护区生产设施的退出和生态恢复工作，促进油田绿色生态文明高质量发展。

Liaohe Oilfield accelerates the withdrawal of production facilities and ecological restoration in the protected areas to promote the high-quality development of the oilfield's green ecological civilization.

截至 2024 年 12 月 5 日，独山子石化塔里木 60 万吨/年乙烷制乙烯项目乙烯年产量达 60.14 万吨，提前 26 天突破设计产量。

As of December 5, 2024, the annual ethylene production of the Dushanzi Petrochemical Tarim 600,000 tons per year ethane to ethylene project reached 601,400 tons, exceeding the designed production 26 days ahead of schedule.

广东石化公司在环保措施上的投资高于国内同类型项目，实现了超低排放。

Guangdong Petrochemical Company has invested more in environmental protection measures than other similar projects in China and has realized ultra-low emissions.

红色南梁碳汇林自 2021 年启动以来，长庆油田与当地政府携手在千亩荒山上种植云杉、油松等乔灌木共计 16.72 万株。

Since the launch of the Red Nanliang Carbon Sink Forest in 2021, Changqing Oilfield and the local government have worked together to plant a total of 167,200 trees and shrubs, such as Picea asperata and Pinus tabuliformis on thousands of mu (a Chinese unit of area) of barren mountains.

为保南疆地区春耕农用化肥供应，塔里木油田塔西南公司开展送化肥下乡服务。

In order to ensure the supply of agricultural fertilizers for spring ploughing in the southern part of Xinjiang, the Taxinan Branch of Tarim Oilfield carried out fertilizer delivery services to rural areas.

中国科学院新疆生态与地理研究所专家（右图）在塔中沙漠植物园观察植被生长情况。这是全球首个建设于大型流动沙漠腹地的植物园，由塔里木油田和中科院新疆生态与地理研究所在塔克拉玛干沙漠中心联合建立。

An expert from the Xinjiang Institute of Ecology and Geography of the Chinese Academy of Sciences, is observing the growth of vegetation in the Tazhong Desert Botanical Garden. This is the world's first botanical garden to be built in the hinterland of a large drifting desert, jointly established in the center of the Taklamakan Desert by Tarim Oilfield and Xinjiang Institute of Ecology and Geography of the Chinese Academy of Sciences.

长庆油田在部署井位时采取避让措施,来保护蓑羽鹤的生存环境。近年来,随着植被的恢复,每年来毛乌素沙地繁衍后代的蓑羽鹤由原来的 20 多只增长到现在的 200 多只。

Changqing Oilfield takes avoidance measures when deploying wells to protect the living environment of the Demoiselle Cranes. In recent years, with the restoration of vegetation, the number of Demoiselle Cranes that come to the Mu Us Sandland to breed each year has increased from more than 20 to over 200 at present.

2024年3月4日，新疆塔克拉玛干沙漠腹地，经过279天的努力，中国石油深地塔科1井钻探深度突破一万米，成为我国首口垂深超过一万米的井，创造了当今世界上钻探一万米深井用时最短纪录。

On March 4, 2024, after 279 days of hard work in the hinterland of the Taklamakan Desert in Xinjiang, the "Well Shendi Take-1" drilled by CNPC reached a depth exceeding 10,000 meters. This achievement marks it as the first well in China to achieve a vertical depth of over 10,000 meters and sets a global record for the shortest time to drill a 10,000-meter deep well.

夏 SUMMER

夏满芒夏暑相连

砥砺之路！照耀着"奔向世界一流"的它具象为脉脉朝晖，是那烈日下的石油热情；比盛夏还酷热的，力尽不知热，但惜夏日长。

广西石化公司坐落于"海上大熊猫"白海豚的故乡——钦州港片区。公司通过引进先进的污水处理系统和浮油回收船,为海洋生物创造了良好的生存环境,白海豚数量从 2004 年的 96 头增至现在的 250 头左右。

Guangxi Petrochemical Company is located in the Qinzhou Port Area, the hometown of the "panda of the sea" white dolphins. By introducing advanced sewage treatment systems and oil recovery vessels, the company has created a favorable living environment for marine life. Consequently, the number of white dolphins has increased from 96 in 2004 to about 250 now.

2023 年 7 月 20 日，我国首次在四川盆地开钻万米深井——"深地川科 1 井"。
On July 20, 2023, for the first time, China drilled a 10,000-meter deep well in the Sichuan Basin, the "Well Shendi Chuanke-1".

广东石化项目投产当年,拉动揭阳市 GDP 从负增长逆袭为广东省增速第一。

In the year when the Guangdong Petrochemical project was commissioned, it pulled Jieyang City's GDP from negative growth to the top growth rate in Guangdong Province.

冀东油田绿色低碳发展成效显著。截至 2024 年底，建成及在建地热供暖项目 14 个，实现供暖面积 2409 万平方米，年减排二氧化碳 146.4 万吨。

Jidong Oilfield has achieved remarkable results in green and low-carbon development. By the end of 2024, 14 geothermal heating projects have been completed and were under construction, realizing a heating area of 24.09 million square meters and an annual emission reduction of 1.464 million tons of carbon dioxide.

中国石油工程建设公司承建的川中油气矿仪陇净化厂光伏及厂内改造工程,在施工中妥善处理施工废料,全天候巡检环保措施落实情况,保护净化厂内外秀美的自然景观。

Photovoltaic and plant renovation projects in the Yilong purification plant of Middle Sichuan Oil & Gas Field, which China Petroleum Engineering & Construction Corp is contracted to build, adequately disposed of construction waste during construction, inspected the implementation of environmental protection measures around the clock, and preserved the beautiful natural landscapes both inside and outside the purification plant.

中国石油入股的卡沙甘油田位于里海东北部,是过去40年世界已发现的最大油田之一。

The Kashagan Oilfield, in which CNPC holds a stake, is located in the northeast of the Caspian Sea. It is one of the largest oilfields discovered in the world over the past 40 years.

掩映在"翠绿"中的西南油气田高石梯中心站。西南油气田构建形成"天然气＋五大业务链"绿色发展西南模式，推动能源结构从"单一化"向"多元化"转变。

The Gaoshiti Central Station of Southwest Oil & Gasfield is covered in "lush green". Southwest Oil & Gasfield has built a "natural gas + five business chains" model, known as the southwest model of green development, which promotes the transformation of the energy structure from "simplification" to "diversification".

山东兰陵县受益于西气东输工程。西气东输送来的天然气，为现代农业种植、农产品深加工、孵化养殖等行业的绿色发展增添了底气。截至 2024 年，西气东输工程已运行 20 年。
Lanling County in Shandong Province is benefiting from the West-East Gas Transmission Project. The natural gas delivered from the project has added confidence to the green development of modern agricultural cultivation, intensive processing of farm produce, incubation and breeding, and other industries. As of 2024, the West-East Gas Transmission Project has been in operation for 20 years.

中国石油首个水面光伏项目——大庆油田星火水面光伏电站，是打造"大庆油田绿色低碳可持续发展示范基地"的先导示范工程。

CNPC's first water surface photovoltaic project is the Daqing Oilfield Starfire Water Surface Photovoltaic Power Station, a pilot project to build the "Daqing Oilfield Green, Low-Carbon, and Sustainable Development Demonstration Base".

长庆油田建成杏子河流域环保示范区，使杏河集输站形成完整伴生气回收利用技术体系，唱响"绿色发展、清洁生产"主旋律。

Changqing Oilfield has built an environmental protection demonstration area in the Xingzi River basin, forming a complete associated gas recovery and utilization technology system in Xinghe Gathering Station, and advocating the theme of "green development and clean production".

1995年，塔克拉玛干沙漠腹地，刚建好的沙漠公路两边寸草不生。

In 1995, in the hinterland of the Taklamakan Desert, there was not an inch of grass on either side of the newly built desert highway.

经过多年建设，500多千米长的塔里木沙漠公路两旁形成了绿色保护长廊，成为全国首条零碳流动性沙漠公路。

After years of construction, the 500-kilometer-long Tarim Desert Highway has formed a green protection corridor on both sides of the highway, making it the first zero-carbon drifting desert highway in China.

中国石油位于川西高原的康定信誉加油站。公司全力打造高原生态环保加油站，推进分布式光伏发电等新能源业务发展，努力构建"低碳能源生态圈"。
CNPC Kangding Xinyu gas station is located in the Western Sichuan Plateau. CNPC is making every effort to build a highland ecological and environmental protection gas station, promoting the development of distributed photovoltaic power generation and other new energy businesses, and endeavoring to establish a "low-carbon energy ecosystem".

大庆油田龙凤湿地自然保护区。2023年,中国石油首批自主贡献型生物多样性保护地落户大庆油田;2024年7月,中国石油首个绿色共享小屋在大庆油田建成开放。

It is Longfeng Wetland Nature Reserve in Daqing Oilfield. In 2023, CNPC's first self-contributing biodiversity reserves were located in Daqing Oilfield. In July 2024, CNPC's first green shared cabin was officially launched in the region.

吉林油田新立采油厂16号大井丛平台,我国首桶零碳原油诞生于此。
Xinli Oil Production Plant No. 16 cluster well platform in Jilin Oilfield is where China's first barrel of zero-carbon crude oil was born.

　　东方物探倾力保护海洋生态环境,在他们的每一艘海上勘探船上都有海洋哺乳动物观察员。他们的主要工作是发现需要保护的野生物种,并监督作业团队是否遵守当地的环保规定。

Bureau of Geophysical Prospecting INC., CNPC (BGP) is committed to protecting the marine ecological environment and has marine mammal observers on each of their offshore exploration vessels. Their main job is to discover wildlife species in need of protection and supervise the operation team to ensure compliance with local environmental regulations.

秋

秋处露秋寒霜降
AUTUMN

与生命的节律同频咬合。石油的齿轮,在秋的深处,大地献出收获的宝藏,秋日将天空铺满金黄,喜看稻菽千重浪,遍地英雄下夕烟。

在华北油田巴彦分公司吉兰泰油区的采油平台处，石油工人紧张忙碌地作业，远处骆驼悠然踱步，构成了一幅和谐画面。

At the oil extraction platform in the Jilantai oil area of Bayan Branch of Huabei Oilfield, petroleum workers are working diligently, and camels are pacing leisurely in the distance, forming a harmonious picture.

冀东油田南堡一号人工岛陆岸终端。这里实行园林属地管理办法,让曾经寸草不生的地方变成绿色家园。
It is the onshore terminal of the No. 1 artificial island in Nanpu, Jidong Oilfield. Here, the garden-style territorial management method is implemented, transforming what was once barren into a green home.

东方物探西南分公司员工在新疆秋里塔格山东秋 6 三维项目施工,在陡崖区攀爬作业,被称为"陡崖飞虎队"。
Employees of the Southwest Branch of BGP were engaged in the construction at Dongqiu-6 3D project in the Qiulitage Mountain area in Xinjiang. They carried out climbing operations in the steep cliff area and were known as the "Flying Tigers on Steep Cliffs".

辽宁盘锦红海滩国家风景廊道旁,辽河油田公司的数十台抽油机排成一道特殊的"风景线"。

Beside the Red Beach National Scenic Corridor in Panjin, Liaoning, dozens of pumping units of Liaohe Oilfield Company are lined up to form a special "scenic view".

长城钻探按照源头绿色化、过程清洁化、防控高效化的总体要求,全力打造清洁高效、低碳循环的绿色井场。

In accordance with the overall requirements of making the source green, the process clean, and the prevention and control highly efficient, Greatwall Drilling has made every effort to build a clean, efficient and low-carbon recycling green well field.

中国石油昆仑物流公司的运输车穿越乌拉山108拐送油到珠峰大本营。
The transport vehicles of CNPC Kunlun Logistics Company Limited crossed the 108 bends of Wula Mountain to deliver oil to the base camp of Mount Qomolangma.

近年来，大港油田因地制宜建设碱蓬草自主贡献型生物多样性保护地，将昔日盐碱荒滩转变为生态湿地公园。
In recent years, Dagang Oilfield has constructed a self-contributing biodiversity conservation area of Suaeda salsa based on the local conditions, transforming the saline-alkali wasteland into an ecological wetland park.

吉林油田国内首个安全零排放的 CCUS-EOR 全流程工业化科技示范项目，如今已平稳运行 10 余年。

The first domestic safety zero-emission CCUS-EOR full-process industrial technology demonstration project in Jilin Oilfield has been running steadily for more than 10 years.

喀土穆炼油厂是苏丹最大的炼油厂,被当地人称为"苏丹的心脏",也是中国石油在非洲的一张靓丽名片。

Khartoum Refinery is the largest oil refinery in Sudan, which is known as "the heart of Sudan" by the locals and a brilliant business card of CNPC in Africa.

中国石油走出海外，除了为当地建设全套石油工业体系外，还积极开展公益活动。例如，中国石油尼日尔公司在当地建造了上百口水井，缓解了当地居民用水难的问题。

CNPC has gone global, not only constructing a complete petroleum industry system for local areas but also actively engaging in public welfare activities. For instance, CNPC Niger Company has built hundreds of water wells locally, alleviating the difficulty of accessing water for local residents.

新加坡是亚洲重要的石油和天然气枢纽。中国石油是新加坡的知名品牌,其加油站数量和零售业务份额分别占到当地市场的 20% 以上。

Singapore is an important oil and gas hub in Asia. CNPC is a well-known brand in Singapore, with the number of gas stations and the share of its retail business accounting for more than 20% of the local market respectively.

巴山蜀水，层林尽染。吉林油田在川南配置区持续优化多种投产模式，加快川南效益建产步伐。

Mountains and Rivers of Sichuan, their serried woods deep-dyed. Jilin Oilfield continues to optimize various investment and production modes in the Chuannan configuration area, accelerating the pace of beneficial construction and production in the south of Sichuan.

　　为保护环境，新疆油田逐步在保护区周边、野生动物迁徙范围地等实施油井退出。在新疆油田各油区内，候鸟迁徙停驻，普氏野马、野驴、鹅喉羚等珍稀动物不时徜徉在油区。

In order to protect the environment, Xinjiang Oilfield has gradually phased out oil wells around protected areas and within wildlife migration areas. In the oil zones of Xinjiang Oilfield, migratory birds have stopped and rare animals such as Przewalski's horses, Asiatic wild asses and Gazella subgutturosas can often be seen roaming the oilfield areas.

塔里木油田克探 103 井生产现场。2024 年以来，塔里木油田锚定天然气 5000 亿立方米增储目标，加快推进新一轮钻完井提速提效革命。

At the production site of the Well Ketan-103 in Tarim Oilfield, since 2024, Tarim Oilfield has set a target of adding 500 billion cubic meters of gas reserves, accelerating a new phase of revolution in speeding up and improving the efficiency of drilling and completion.

新疆的油气田企业秉持"开发一个区块,保护一片绿洲,撑起一片蓝天"的理念,使作业区附近的野生动物种群不断扩大、物种不断丰富,生态功能稳步趋好。
The oil and gas field enterprises in Xinjiang uphold the concept of "developing a block, protecting an oasis, and supporting a blue sky", ensuring that wildlife populations near the operation areas continue to grow, species diversity increases, and ecological functions steadily improve.

吉林油田华侨风电场,是中国石油第一个自消纳全容量并网发电的风电场。

The Huaqiao Wind Farm in Jilin Oilfield is the first self-consuming full-capacity grid-connected generation wind farm of CNPC.

冬

冬雪雪冬小大寒 WINTER

为每个冬日写下最后的句点!他们用石油工业的春暖花开,点染出独属于自己的热血丹青;以寒为笔,以雪作画,石油人在白色荒原,千里冰封,万里雪飘。

油城盘锦，近处的抽油机与远处的炼塔交相辉映。
In the oil city of Panjin, the nearby pumping units and the distant refinery towers complement each other, creating a striking scene.

西南油气田龙王庙的雪原小站。西南油气田连续 10 年天然气产量实现年均近 30 亿立方米快速增长,将丰厚的资源潜力化为惠及一方的"福气"。

It is the station at Longwang Temple in Southwest Oil & Gas Field. Southwest Oil & Gas Field has achieved annual average growth of nearly 3 billion cubic meters of natural gas production for several consecutive years, turning its abundant resource potential into "blessings" for the benefit of the local community.

被大雪覆盖的博孜天然气处理厂。这里处理的天然气会进入西气东输管网，源源不断奔向我国东部，福泽上亿百姓。

It is the snow-covered Bozi Gas Processing Plant. The natural gas processed here will enter the West-East Gas Pipeline network and run continuously to the eastern part of China, benefiting hundreds of millions of people.

辽河油田月东项目部人工岛生产现场。这个项目部管理着我国首座采用稠油热采方式开发的海上油田。
It is the production site of artificial island in the Yuedong Project Department of the Liaohe Oilfield. This project department operates China's first offshore oil field, which was developed through heavy oil thermal recovery technology.

大庆油田古龙页岩油示范区大型压裂现场。该示范区地处松辽盆地北部，将成为大庆百年油田建设的重要资源地。
It is the large-scale fracturing site in Gulong Shale Oil Demonstration Area of Daqing Oilfield. This demonstration area is located in the northern part of the Songliao Basin and will become an important resource site for the sustainable development of Daqing.

塔里木油田因地制宜推进油气田生产用能清洁替代。截至 2024 年 10 月初，塔里木油田今年光伏项目累计发电突破 10 亿千瓦时，相当于替代标煤 30 万吨。
Tarim Oilfield has been advancing clear energy substitution for oil and gas production energy use through localized approaches. By early October 2024, the cumulative electricity generation of PV projects in Tarim Oilfield this year has exceeded 1 billion kW·h, equivalent to replacing 300,000 tons of standard coal.

虎林—长春天然气管道工程施工现场。宝石管业公司统筹"产供销储运"等环节，为油气勘探开发、重点管道建设、社会民生项目等发运各类优质管材。
It is the construction site of the Hulin-Changchun natural gas pipeline project. Baoji Petroleum Pipe Industry Co., Ltd. coordinates the entire chain of production, supply, marketing, storage, and transportation to deliver a variety of high-quality pipes for oil and gas exploration and development, key pipeline construction, and public welfare projects.

海拔 3500 米的尕斯库勒油田。近年来，青海油田坚持"做大新能源"战略举措不动摇，加快打造油气与新能源产业高地。
The Gasikule Oilfield is located at an altitude of 3,500 meters. In recent years, Qinghai Oilfield has been committed to the strategic initiative of "expanding new energy" and has expedited the development of a highland of oil, gas, and new energy industry.

中国石油江苏 LNG 接收站是长三角地区调峰能力最强的接收站，其生产的天然气惠及华东、长三角地区近 2 亿人口。
CNPC's Jiangsu LNG terminal is the receiving terminal with the strongest peaking capacity in the Yangtze River Delta area, and the natural gas it produces benefits nearly 200 million people in East China and the Yangtze River Delta area.

柯尔克孜族老人拉着中国石油员工的手行吻手礼（右图），感谢石油人通过南疆天然气利民工程将"福气"送到帕米尔高原。该工程是中国石油提高当地群众生活水平、保护生态环境的一项民生工程。

The elderly kirgiz man is performing a hand-kissing gesture of respect and gratitude while holding the hand of a CNPC's employee. This gesture is indicative of gratitude for the workers bringing "fortune" to the Pamir Plateau through the Beneficial Project of the south of Xinjiang. This project is a livelihood project of CNPC to improve the living standard of local people and protect the ecological environment.

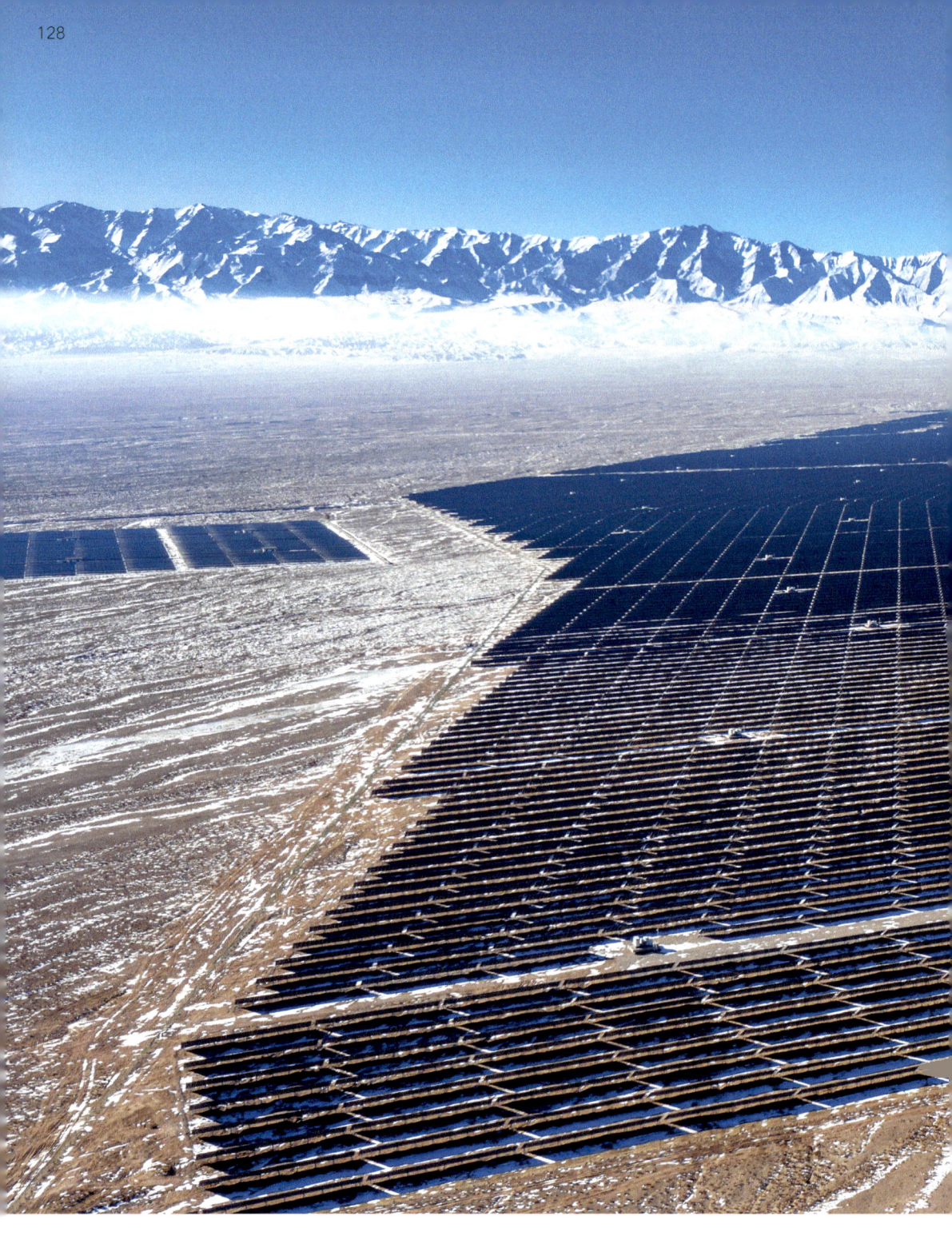

中国石油首个集中式光伏电站——玉门油田200兆瓦光伏示范项目。

CNPC's first centralized photovoltaic power station: the Yumen Oilfield 200 MW photovoltaic demonstration project.

东方物探员工在西秋里塔格区块进行山地勘探作业。
Employees of BGP carried out mountain exploration operations in the West Qiulitage block.